WOULD YOU RATHER?

EASTER
EDITION

RIDDLELAND

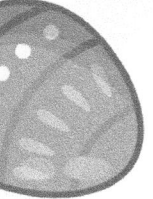

TABLE OF CONTENTS

INTRODUCTION

Welcome to a world where every corner hides a surprise, every egg holds a secret, and every choice leads to a brand-new burst of Easter fun! This book is packed with 300 playful, imaginative, and sometimes wonderfully weird Would You Rather? questions that turn the Easter season into an adventure you can enjoy anytime, anywhere.

Easter is already full of magic: colorful eggs, chocolate bunnies, spring sunshine, and that special feeling that something exciting is about to happen. But inside these pages, Easter grows even bigger. Here, eggs can glow, candy can talk, and bunnies have entire towns buzzing with silly inventions and carrot-powered machines. With every question, you'll hop into a new scene bursting with laughter and creativity.

You'll make choices like: Will you go on a wild egg hunt where the eggs keep running away? Will you visit Bunny Town and meet bunnies with the most unexpected jobs? Will you try a candy flavor so strange you can't decide if you're brave or just... curious?

The joy of this book is simple: there are no wrong answers. Every choice reveals something funny, surprising, or imaginative, especially when you play with family or friends. Kids love explaining why they chose Option A instead of Option B, and grown-ups often discover the explanations are even sillier than the questions.

You can play at home, on a car ride, at an Easter party, in the classroom, or while waiting for the big egg hunt to begin. Wherever you are, this book brings instant Easter cheer, plenty of laughter, and moments your family will remember long after the chocolate has disappeared.

So grab your basket, warm up your imagination, and hop into a world where springtime magic never ends.

Your Easter fun begins... right now.

HOW TO PLAY

Get ready to hop into a world of silly choices, magical eggs, and Easter fun! This book is filled with 300 laugh-out-loud Would You Rather? questions designed to spark imagination, inspire giggles, and bring families together.

Playing is super easy; here's how it works:

1. Choose Your Players
Play with your family, your friends, your classmates... or even by yourself. Whether you've got a whole Easter party or just one curious bunny, the game works every time.

2. Pick a Question
Flip to any page and read a question aloud. Each one gives you two funny, magical, or totally unexpected choices.
Example: Would you rather ride in the Easter Bunny's carrot-powered car... OR fly on a giant jelly-bean rocket?

3. Make Your Choice
Everyone picks the option they like best. There are no right or wrong answers here; only the most hilarious ones you can come up with.

4. Share Your Reasons (Optional, but So Much Better!)
Explaining why you chose your answer often leads to the biggest laughs. Sometimes the story behind your choice is even sillier than the choice itself!

5. Play Just for Fun... or Turn It Into a Game
You can keep it simple and enjoy the questions, or add a competitive twist: Everyone who chooses Option A gets 1 point. Everyone who chooses Option B gets 1 point. Play 10 questions and see who wins, or make your own Easter-themed rules.

6. Try Special Easter Rounds
Make the game even more exciting with optional challenge modes:
- Bunny Hop Round: You must answer while hopping in place!
- Speed Egg Round: You have 3 seconds to choose; no thinking!
- Mystery Basket Round: Close your eyes, flip the book open, and point. That's your question.

7. Play Anywhere
This book travels well! Play at home, on a road trip, at an Easter gathering, during a family dinner, or even while waiting for the big egg hunt to begin. No matter how you play, get ready for giggles, surprises, and unforgettable Easter moments. Let's crack open the fun; your adventure starts now!

CHAPTER 1

WELCOME TO THE EASTER WONDERLAND

Step inside the Easter Wonderland: the place where spring wakes up, colors sparkle a little brighter, and even the air smells like fresh flowers and chocolate. This is the moment when Easter magic begins to peek out from behind every corner. Bunnies hop a little faster. Chicks chirp a little louder. And eggs… well, they're never quite where you expect them to be.

In this chapter, you're taking your very first hop into a world where the ordinary becomes extraordinary, where a simple walk outside might lead you to a glowing egg, a silly bunny parade, or a trail of jelly-beans that absolutely did not exist yesterday.

Every question here is designed to open the door to this magical world gently: helping you warm up your imagination, loosen your giggles, and get ready for the sillier, wilder Easter adventures waiting in the rest of the book.

So take a deep breath of springtime air, grab your imaginary bunny ears, and let your creativity stretch like a chick breaking out of its shell.

Welcome to Easter Wonderland, where the fun begins the moment you choose your first "Would You Rather?"

Would you rather
hop like a bunny everywhere
you go for a whole day,  leave a trail of
tiny glitter eggs behind
every step?

Would you rather
have the Easter Bunny
deliver all your messages,  have a fluffy chick
be your personal
snack waiter?

Would you rather
smell like a bouquet
of spring flowers wherever
you walk  smell like freshly melted
chocolate all week long?

Would you rather
discover a glowing mini-egg
no bigger than a marble  a giant rainbow-painted
egg that's taller
than your bed?

Would you rather
have a cuddly bunny follow
you like a loyal sidekick  a tiny lamb
that thinks you're
its hero?

Would you rather own a basket
that magically refills with your favorite Easter treats,

or have a helpful Easter bunny
that cleans your whole room the moment you blink?

Would you rather
bounce on a trampoline
made of marshmallow Peeps

OR

ride down a slide
made of warm,
flowing chocolate?

Would you rather have a talking bunny who tells funny stories  a chick that performs tiny magic tricks with sparkly feathers?

Would you rather decorate eggs that float around you like planets  eggs that change patterns every time you laugh?

Would you rather wear shoes that chirp like chicks with every step  a hat that pops open and releases bouncing Easter eggs?

Would you rather discover a hidden bunny door in your home that leads to a secret tunnel,  find a nest of enchanted eggs in your backyard that open only at sunset?

Would you rather live in a neighborhood where every tree grows jelly-beans  one where every bush grows chocolate eggs?

Would you rather own a magic paintbrush
that transforms any egg design instantly,

or a wand that summons
a brand-new Easter basket whenever you wave it?

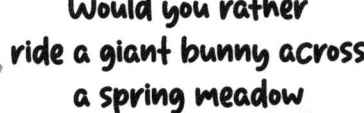

Would you rather
ride a giant bunny across
a spring meadow

OR

soar through the sky
on a spinning, sparkling
Easter egg?

Would you rather carry a carrot-shaped flashlight that glows extra bright  an egg-shaped gadget that tells silly jokes?

Would you rather wake up to a room decorated like the most colorful Easter morning ever  step outside to find your backyard turned into a giant, twisty egg maze?

Would you rather have a friendly bunny family move in next door  a whole flock of cheerful chicks that greet you every morning?

Would you rather hear bunnies whispering goofy secrets whenever you pass them,  hear chicks singing tiny cheerful songs all day?

Would you rather leave a trail of blooming spring flowers behind you  a trail of sparkling mini-eggs every time you move?

Would you rather open your backpack
and find it stuffed with candy eggs,

or open it and discover
dozens of fluffy chicks ready to cuddle?

Would you rather
challenge the Easter Bunny
to a hopping race

OR

play hide-and-seek with
him in a giant garden filled
with magical hiding spots?

Would you rather
have a spring breeze that
helps you jump twice as high  one that helps you
run twice as fast?

Would you rather
eat an egg-shaped treat
the size of your head  a chocolate bunny
as tall as you are?

Would you rather
help the Easter Bunny
pack baskets in his
magical workshop  help decorate Bunny
Town for its annual
Spring Parade?

Would you rather
own a basket that plays
cheerful music when
you shake it,  eggs that burst into
laughter whenever
you tap them?

Would you rather
explore a field of
bouncing jelly-beans  a garden of
talking tulips that
tell terrible jokes?

Would you rather have a tiny chick that rides on your shoulder everywhere,  a bunny that loves hiding inside your hoodie pocket?

Would you rather have your shadow look like a hopping bunny  sound like a chirping chick whenever you walk?

Would you rather discover a magical egg that tells funny stories  one that predicts silly things that will happen later in your day?

Would you rather start every morning with a colorful, dancing Easter Parade  a giant breakfast feast filled with every Easter treat imaginable?

CHAPTER 2

THE ULTIMATE EASTER EGG HUNT

Welcome to the greatest egg hunt of your life; a place where eggs don't just hide… they escape, wiggle, float, glow, and sometimes team up to outsmart you. Trails sparkle, clues whisper, and every corner is packed with surprises waiting to be discovered.

Grab your basket, warm up your hopping legs, and step into a hunt where every choice leads to another burst of Easter magic. Ready? The chase begins now!

Would you rather chase eggs that keep rolling away like runaway marbles  eggs that bounce higher every time you get close?

Would you rather find an egg hidden inside a drifting cloud  tucked deep inside a patch of giggling tulips?

Would you rather use a basket that lights up when an egg is nearby  one that makes a "ding!" whenever an egg is within ten steps?

Would you rather hunt for eggs in a giant twisty maze  in a forest where the trees whisper clues in silly rhymes?

Would you rather discover one huge glittering golden egg  ten tiny rainbow eggs that burst into giggles when you grab them?

Would you rather track down eggs that flutter around like butterflies  ones that vanish and reappear in random spots?

Would you rather climb onto a floating island full of hidden eggs  crawl inside a giant hollow chocolate bunny to search for secret treasures?

Would you rather hunt invisible eggs you can only hear jingling,  glowing eggs that keep zipping away like mini rockets?

Would you rather climb a towering marshmallow mountain to snag an egg  cross a wobbly jelly-bean bridge to reach one?

Would you rather pick up an egg that challenges you with riddles  one that dares you to do silly Easter stunts?

Would you rather
follow a bunny guide who gives twisted clues

or a chick guide
who blurts out clues too early?

Would you rather
find eggs that
constantly shift colors

 **OR** eggs that slowly transform
into funny shapes?

Would you rather race a friend to find the first hidden egg  team up to locate the hardest-to-find egg in the whole hunt?

Would you rather grab an egg perched on a giant sunflower  one hidden beneath a rock that giggles loudly when touched?

Would you rather your basket shrink smaller with every egg you collect,  grow hilariously giant every time you drop one?

Would you rather hunt while hopping everywhere like a bunny  while marching in slow-motion like a dramatic Easter robot?

Would you rather discover an egg that unlocks hidden doors  one that turns into a tiny glowing lantern?

Would you rather
search on a windy hill where eggs zoom away,

or in a quiet meadow
where eggs slowly sink into fluffy grass?

Would you rather
catch an egg that floats
a little higher every time
you jump,

OR

one that shrinks
smaller every time you
take a step?

Would you rather find an egg tucked in a bird's nest above your head  hidden in a cozy burrow beneath your feet?

Would you rather pick up an egg that sings your favorite song,  one that copies whatever sound you make, even the silly ones?

Would you rather your basket make loud chicken clucks every time you score an egg,  bunny-hopping sounds every time you get near one?

Would you rather have 10 minutes to collect as many eggs as possible,  a whole hour to find one egg hidden unbelievably well?

Would you rather grab an egg that feels icy cold  one that's warm and fuzzy like a tiny baby chick?

Would you rather
find an egg inside a giant carrot house

or hidden somewhere
in a magical mushroom village?

Would you rather
follow a trail of shimmering
Easter sparkles that might
lead to a hidden egg

OR

chase bunny paw
prints that vanish right
before your eyes?

Would you rather discover an egg that opens a secret underground tunnel  an egg that reveals a cozy treehouse hideout?

Would you rather chase an egg that hops away unless you whisper nicely,  one that freezes only when you shout "STOP!" very dramatically?

Would you rather have an Easter egg hunt during a magical rain shower that makes everything sparkle,  a breezy day where clues drift through the air?

Would you rather complete the egg hunt to unlock a giant mystery basket  reveal a secret Easter map that leads to something even bigger?

CHAPTER 3:

CANDY CHAOS & CHOCOLATE SURPRISES

Welcome to the sweetest corner of Easter Wonderland: a place where chocolate rivers shimmer under spring sunshine, jelly-bean trees shake with flavor, and marshmallows bounce higher than you can jump. Here, every treat has a personality, a secret talent, or a mischievous plan of its own.

Grab your spoon, your sweet tooth, and maybe a napkin… because things are about to get deliciously out of control.

Would you rather bite into a chocolate bunny that cracks jokes nonstop  a marshmallow chick that sings catchy songs you can't stop humming?

Would you rather eat a jelly-bean that changes your voice into silly characters,  a chocolate egg that changes your hair color every hour?

Would you rather swim in a warm river of melted chocolate  bounce on a marshmallow trampoline that launches you into the air?

Would you rather discover a new jelly-bean flavor each morning  a candy that magically refills every time you take a bite?

Would you rather carry an Easter basket that refills with your favorite candy only when you laugh,  an Easter basket that creates brand-new mystery flavors?

Would you rather have a chocolate bunny friend
who gives you daily challenges

or a gummy chick friend
who dares you to try outrageous flavors?

Would you rather
try a jelly-bean labeled
"SUPER STRANGE"

OR

a chocolate egg labeled
"SUPER MAGICAL"?

Would you rather open an Easter basket that explodes with surprise candies  discover a chocolate tree covered in gooey Easter treats?

Would you rather jelly-beans grow like flowers in your yard  chocolate eggs fall from the sky whenever you dance?

Would you rather eat a sour Easter egg that makes you float like a balloon  a spicy jelly-bean that sends your legs hopping like the Easter Bunny?

Would you rather unwrap a chocolate egg that reveals a magical key  one that reveals a tiny living candy animal?

Would you rather unwrap chocolate eggs that whisper secrets nonstop  jelly-beans that vanish the moment you laugh?

Would you rather
your tongue turn rainbow every time you eat candy,

or glow neon like
a glow stick in the dark?

Would you rather
battle a giant chocolate
bunny in
a hip-hop dance-off

OR

a giant Easter chick in a
joke-telling showdown?

Would you rather taste a jelly-bean that tastes like cheesy pizza  one that tastes like sparkly fresh rainbows?

Would you rather live in a fort made of cracked chocolate Easter eggs  a squishy jelly-bean hut that jiggles every time the Easter Bunny hops by?

Would you rather have unlimited chocolate that melts instantly,  unlimited jelly-beans that bounce away unless you trap them?

Would you rather discover a fountain that sprays chocolate milk  a fountain that hiccups fizzy jelly-beans and candy bubbles?

Would you rather carry an Easter egg basket, where the dyed eggs change different colors and patterns  wear a daffodil crown that makes baskets refill with surprises?

Would you rather
eat a jelly-bean the size of your head

or a chocolate bunny as tall
as your entire body?

Would you rather
try an egg filled with
creamy pudding

OR

one filled with
warm caramel goo?

Would you rather jump through bubbles that smell like chocolate  stomp on confetti that pops into tiny jelly-beans?

Would you rather meet a marshmallow chick that squeaks and melts in the sun  a jelly-bean-covered bunny that sheds candy as it hops?

Would you rather chew pastel Easter gum that makes giant bunny-shaped bubbles,  gum that floats you over the grass while you hunt for eggs?

Would you rather eat a magical Easter egg that causes glittery hiccups every few seconds,  a jelly-bean treat that makes you sneeze tiny bunny-shaped beans?

Would you rather eat an egg that tastes totally different with every bite,  one that lasts forever and never, ever loses its flavor?

Would you rather eat a chocolate bunny that gives you super strength for five minutes, allowing you to carry all the full Easter baskets you can find  eat a handful of jelly-beans that give you super speed and allow you to complete Easter egg hunts in under 3 minutes?

Would you rather nibble on chocolate that giggles every time you bite it,  jelly-beans that wiggle around your hand?

Would you rather eat a candy egg that whispers secret messages  one that teaches you a new silly song?

Would you rather win a lifetime supply of your favorite candy  unlock a map to the hidden Candy Kingdom where everything, yes, everything, is edible?

CHAPTER 4:
BUNNY TOWN ADVENTURES

Welcome to Bunny Town, the heart of Easter Wonderland; a cheerful little place where bunnies don't just hop… they hustle! Carrot factories puff out sweet-smelling clouds, bunny engineers test inventions that usually wobble before they work, and shopkeepers greet you with fluffy tails wiggling in excitement. Every street is alive with color: egg-shaped lanterns, carrot-shaped vehicles, and bunnies practicing for festivals happening almost every day.

Take a stroll through town, lend a paw to its busy residents, and get ready for some truly hare-raising choices.

Would you rather help a bunny mail carrier deliver Easter cards and egg-shaped packages around Bunny Town,  help a bunny baker frost towering carrot-cake cupcakes for the Easter celebration?

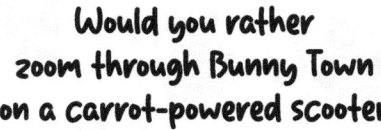

Would you rather zoom through Bunny Town on a carrot-powered scooter  float above it in an Easter basket-shaped blimp piloted by tiny chicks?

Would you rather tour Bunny Town's legendary egg-painting studio, where colors magically swirl,  visit the carrot candy factory where every treat wiggles before you eat it?

Would you rather have a bunny teacher who uses egg hunts to teach math  one who turns every lesson into a hopping Easter dance??

Would you rather help a bunny mechanic fix a squeaky carrot racecar for the Bunny Town Easter parade,  test an egg-shaped robot that randomly launches dyed eggs during the egg hunt?

Would you rather attend a bunny talent show where rabbits hop over giant Easter eggs,  one where they juggle glowing eggs that giggle when dropped?

Would you rather live in a chocolate bunny-shaped house that smells sweet all day  an Easter egg-shaped house that changes colors every morning?

Would you rather have a bunny neighbor who drops off fresh Easter treats and chocolate eggs every morning,  one who brings a new box of marshmallow chicks every day that squeak when you squeeze them?

Would you rather learn how to sculpt chocolate Easter bunnies into tiny masterpieces  learn to paint eggs that come alive and dance?

Would you rather explore a bunny library where Easter stories pop open with eggs, chicks and spring magic,  a bunny arcade filled with egg-launching games?

Would you rather join the Bunny Town
marching band with carrot trumpets

or the bunny hop-dance crew
with glowing tail costumes?

Would you rather
be chased down Carrot
Boulevard by an angry
Hot Cross Bun

OR

by an egg-delivery
wagon spilling dyed eggs
as it rolls?

Would you rather help the Bunny Town mayor plan the giant Easter Parade  help the bunny police track down a gang of mischievous jelly-bean bandits?

Would you rather order a warm cup of hot chocolate from a bunny barista  a marshmallow muffin from the town's fluffiest baker?

Would you rather help Bunny Town lambs decorate the playground with daffodils, ribbons, and hidden eggs,  fill the water fountain with swirling multi-colored egg-dye so that people can dip their Easter eggs in there?

Would you rather have a pet bunny that roller-skates through the Easter egg hunt,  one whose ears magically pull dyed eggs, candy, and flowers out of thin air?

Would you rather join a Bunny Town workshop where bunnies build gadgets powered by jelly-beans and Easter candy,  a training class on controlling magical bouncing eggs?

Would you rather soak in
a Bunny Town spa bubbling with melted chocolate eggs

or leave a salon with a tail
so fluffy it bounces like a marshmallow chick?

Would you rather
hop everywhere like
a real bunny while in town,

 **OR**

wear bunny slippers
that squeak loudly every
time you take a step?

Would you rather work delivering Easter eggs  build custom baskets in the Easter workshop?

Would you rather be Bunny Town's official Easter balloon blower, filling giant egg-shaped balloons for parades and egg hunts,  smashing a giant chocolate egg to open every new store?

Would you rather watch a Bunny Town Easter circus where bunnies bounce on giant jelly-bean eggs and launch themselves into baskets,  a trapeze show where bunnies have to catch bouncing eggs mid-air without dropping them?

Would you rather ride Bunny Town's carrot monorail that hands out Easter eggs at every stop,  call a taxi shaped like a giant decorated egg?

Would you rather play egg-bouncing soccer with bunnies  jelly-bean basketball where the balls keep shifting colors?

Would you rather solve missing
Easter egg mysteries with Detective Floppy Ears

or deliver surprise Easter treats
with Captain Carrot Crunch on his carrot cycle?

Would you rather
help decorate Bunny Town
for the Spring Glow Festival

OR

paint glowing eggs for the
Midnight Egg Parade?

Would you rather stroll down Hot Cross Bun Lane, where the air smells sweet and spicy,

Eggshell Avenue, where painted Easter eggs sparkle and crunch softly under your shoes?

Would you rather get your hair styled by a Bunny Town barber using sparkly egg-shaped hair clips and pastel ribbons,

receive Easter face paint from a bunny artist who draws bouncing chicks and hopping eggs that wiggle?

Would you rather compete in Bunny Town's Egg Balancing Olympics

race in the Great Easter Egg Roll, chasing wobbling painted eggs down the bouncy hills?

Would you rather be in charge of Bunny Town's Easter Egg Hunt and Spring Festival for a day,

become the official Egg Tester who gets to try every new treat before anyone else?

CHAPTER 5:
EGG DECORATING MAYHEM

Welcome to the Egg Decorating Pavilion, the most chaotic and creative workshop in all of Easter Wonderland! Here, paintbrushes hover in mid-air waiting for instructions, rainbow dyes bubble with excitement, and glitter storms swirl without warning. Some eggs behave nicely… most do not. They wiggle, hum, float, and occasionally try to decorate themselves.

Today, you're not just decorating eggs: you're stepping into a whirlwind of color, magic, and laugh-out-loud surprises.

Ready? Take a deep breath… and step into the mayhem.

Would you rather decorate eggs that float around you in tiny orbits  eggs that spin faster every time you try to touch them?

Would you rather use paint that changes colors with each brush stroke  glitter that creates sparkles big enough to light up the whole room?

Would you rather work with eggs that giggle when you pick them up  eggs that hum a goofy tune while you decorate them?

Would you rather paint one giant egg taller than you are,  decorate one hundred mini eggs that keep zipping across the table?

Would you rather hold a magic brush that paints flawless designs by itself,  a wand that adds decorations you didn't expect at all?

Would you rather
dip your egg into a roaring rainbow river

or spray it with enchanted cloud mist
that makes mystery patterns appear?

Would you rather
decorate eggs that glow
like neon signs

 **OR**

eggs that shimmer
like mirrors when you shine
light on them?

Would you rather paint eggs whose patterns dance across the shell  eggs whose designs wiggle every time you shake them?

Would you rather decorate an egg that politely requests colors  one that loudly complains whenever you pick the wrong shade?

Would you rather decorate eggs in a gravity-free room where everything floats,  in a bounce room where everything hops around you?

Would you rather use dye that smells like freshly baked chocolate  paint that releases a burst of spring flower scent?

Would you rather work with a paintbrush that laughs uncontrollably  glue that tries to wriggle off the table every two minutes?

Would you rather create eggs
that light up when you clap your hands

or eggs that play silly sound effects
when you tilt them?

Would you rather
design eggs that sprout
tiny fluttering wings

eggs that grow soft,
fluffy tails?

Would you rather decorate eggs that slowly spin above your head  eggs that roll behind you like loyal pets?

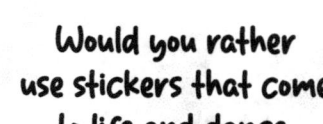

Would you rather use stickers that come to life and dance,  ribbons that whip themselves into perfect bows?

Would you rather paint eggs that whisper silly secrets  eggs that laugh loudly when you tickle them with a brush?

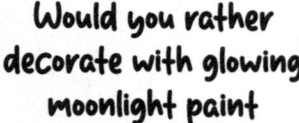

Would you rather decorate with glowing moonlight paint  with sparkling sunrise dust that warms the whole room?

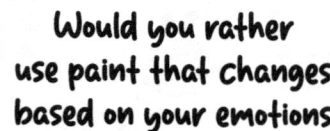

Would you rather use paint that changes based on your emotions  dye that transforms based on the sounds around you?

Would you rather decorate
a fragile crystal egg that sparkles beautifully

or a super-bouncy rubber egg
that refuses to hold still?

Would you rather
make eggs that smell
like sweet candy

eggs that smell like
fresh spring rain
after a storm?

Would you rather decorate eggs in a room filled with floating feathers drifting around you  in a room swirling with soft, magical sparkles?

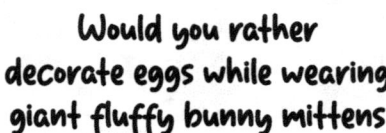

Would you rather decorate eggs while wearing giant fluffy bunny mittens  while hopping nonstop like an excited bunny?

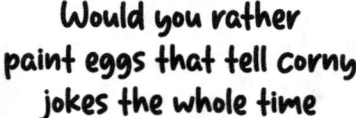

Would you rather paint eggs that tell corny jokes the whole time  eggs that keep asking you tricky riddles?

Would you rather decorate eggs that twirl like ballerinas  eggs that glow, hover, and follow you around?

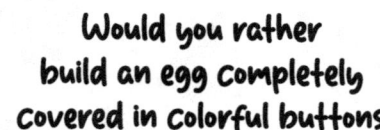

Would you rather build an egg completely covered in colorful buttons  one wrapped entirely in fancy ribbons and bows?

Would you rather decorate eggs that open into magical mini-scenes  eggs that glow brighter every time someone smiles near them?

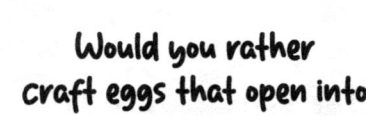

Would you rather craft eggs that open into tiny pop-up stories  eggs that project colorful pictures on the walls?

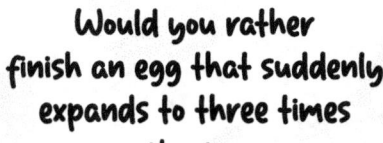

Would you rather finish an egg that suddenly expands to three times its size  one that shrinks into a pocket-sized charm?

Would you rather decorate the legendary Grand Festival Egg that all of Easter Wonderland will admire,  craft a secret magical egg that only you will ever know exists?

CHAPTER 6:
MAGICAL EASTER CREATURES

Welcome to the enchanted outskirts of Easter Wonderland, a shimmering place where magic hums in the air and every creature has a story. Here, baby chicks hatch with glow-in-the-dark feathers, bunnies learn spells before they learn to hop, unicorns doodle rainbows across the sky, and dragons roast marshmallows with gentle spark-breath.

Some creatures are brave. Some are curious. Some are so mischievous they can't go five minutes without causing magical chaos. But all of them are eager to meet you.

Take a deep breath… The enchanted creatures of Easter Wonderland are ready for your next adventure.

Would you rather have a talking bunny sidekick who casts tiny spells with its whiskers  a baby dragon who can toast marshmallows with cute puffs of glittery heat?

Would you rather ride a jelly-bean unicorn that leaves candy trails behind it  a rainbow llama that floats a few inches above the ground when it walks?

Would you rather adopt a chick that glows different colors depending on its mood  a bunny whose ears predict the weather by wiggling in funny ways?

Would you rather have a magical egg that hatches into a brand-new creature every day,  an egg that hatches into one mysterious creature you've never seen before?

Would you rather fly through the sky on a giant pastel owl with soft, sparkling feathers  bounce across the clouds on a fluffy sky-sheep?

Would you rather train a shy Easter egg-dragon who only breathes colorful confetti puffs  a clumsy marshmallow unicorn whose sugary tail keeps sticking to everything, including you?

Would you rather meet a Marshmallow Puff Bunny who paints rainbow paths with its cotton-candy tail  a Glitter Chick who sneezes shimmering sparkles instead of chirping?

Would you rather explore a glowing forest filled with magical bunnies  a sparkling meadow where mythical chicks dance in circles?

Would you rather have a creature that can shape-shift into anything you need,  one that can clone itself into silly duplicates?

Would you rather travel with a bunny who can dig tunnels anywhere  a fox who can open tiny portals to surprise locations?

Would you rather meet a rabbit wizard
who turns carrots into treasure

or a chick alchemist who brews potions
that smell like bubblegum?

Would you rather
have a talking egg that
gives dramatic advice

OR

a floating chick
who insists it's the leader
of your adventures?

Would you rather help a Jelly-bean Bunny find its hidden candy burrow  help a shy Sparkle Chick recover the glowing Easter egg it accidentally misplaced?

Would you rather care for a creature that grows bigger every time you laugh  shrinks smaller every time you sneeze?

Would you rather have a bunny that can teleport a few feet at a time,  a chick that can stop time for exactly five seconds?

Would you rather team up with a creature that controls soft breezes  one that can summon gentle spring rain showers?

Would you rather race across the fields on a lightning-fast hare  glide through the sky on a rainbow-feathered Easter chick?

Would you rather learn to fly
from a giant butterfly instructor

or learn to swim from a magical mer-bunny
with a sparkly tail?

Would you rather
hatch an egg that sings
lullabies every night

OR

one that tells silly stories
whenever you ask?

Would you rather have a creature that brings you a tiny good-luck charm each morning  one that grants one teeny-tiny wish each day?

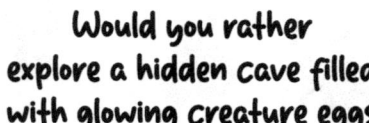

Would you rather explore a hidden cave filled with glowing creature eggs  climb a mountain where rare magical animals gather at sunrise?

Would you rather befriend a bunny with invisible fur you can only see in moonlight,  a chick whose feathers change color with every step?

Would you rather live near a magical pond where frogs speak poetry  near a meadow where glowing caterpillars light up the night?

Would you rather babysit a hyper fluffy lamb who can't sit still,  a sleepwalking Easter bunny who keeps wandering into sparkly places?

Would you rather discover a map
that leads to a valley of forgotten creatures

or a key that unlocks
a secret creature sanctuary?

Would you rather
have a creature that
makes you float when
you're excited

OR

glow brightly
when you're nervous?

Would you rather rescue a creature trapped inside a giant, enchanted egg  one stuck in a topsy-turvy, upside-down world?

Would you rather have a creature companion who loves daring adventures  one who loves causing harmless magical chaos?

Would you rather hatch a creature that can read minds  one that can speak every language - even butterfly?

Would you rather become the honorary Guardian of All Magical Creatures  the official Easter Wonderland Egg Hatcher for every rare creature born?

CHAPTER 7:
SILLY EASTER DISASTERS

Welcome to the wildest corner of Easter Wonderland, the place where everything tries to behave… but absolutely never does.

Chocolate rivers suddenly rise like tidal waves, runaway eggs roll through town like they're training for the Egg Olympics, glitter storms swirl out of nowhere, and one unlucky sneeze can trigger a magical chain reaction. Even the Easter Bunny himself avoids this part of town unless he's wearing safety goggles.

But here's the fun part: every disaster comes with laughter, every accident turns into a story, and every "uh-oh" leads straight to adventure. Step carefully, hold onto your basket, and get ready for some wonderfully wacky Easter mayhem!

Would you rather chase a chocolate bunny that melts faster the closer you get,  a marshmallow chick that bounces higher every time it laughs?

Would you rather slip on a road suddenly paved with jelly-beans  get stuck in enchanted grass that grows taller every time you wiggle?

Would you rather your Easter basket sprout legs and hop away,  suddenly start spinning like a helicopter taking off?

Would you rather get caught in a glowing glitter tornado  drenched in a sticky-but-sweet jelly-bean shower?

Would you rather watch a giant egg crack open into a confetti explosion  into a flood of squeaking baby chicks?

Would you rather be chased
by one huge egg rolling down a hill

or by twenty-two tiny eggs moving in perfect,
spooky formation?

Would you rather
a magic paintbrush go
wild and decorate you
instead of the eggs,

OR

glue that sticks
everything together...
including your shadow?

Would you rather
your bunny ears suddenly
inflate like balloons  shrink until they look like
tiny raisin-sized nubs?

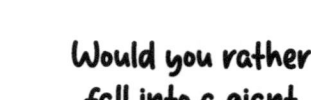

Would you rather
fall into a giant
marshmallow pit  slip straight into a deep
caramel puddle?

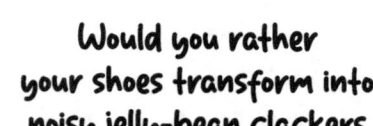

Would you rather
your shoes transform into
noisy jelly-bean clackers  into squeaky chick slippers
with every step?

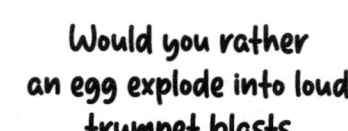

Would you rather
an egg explode into loud
trumpet blasts  into a disco beat that
forces you to dance
uncontrollably?

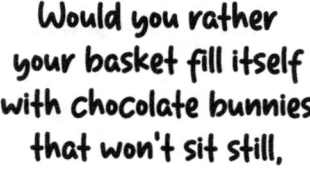

Would you rather
your basket fill itself
with chocolate bunnies
that won't sit still,  jelly-beans
that bounce out
the second you blink?

Would you rather accidentally
grow a carrot as big as your house

or accidentally hatch
an egg that zooms away at rocket speed?

Would you rather
try to reverse a spell
that turned your hair into
cotton candy

OR

one that made you
smell like a giant
jelly-bean jar?

Would you rather retrieve an egg stuck on the highest rooftop  fish one out of the bubbling center of a chocolate fountain?

Would you rather your socks turn into springy grass that hops on its own,  into chick slippers that chirp loudly every time you move?

Would you rather have a chocolate river suddenly rush your way like a sweet tsunami  a swirling tornado of feathers spinning toward you?

Would you rather an egg burst open and shout embarrassing jokes,  burst open and command everyone around you to dance?

Would you rather fall through a portal into Upside-Down Easterland  tumble into a maze dug by mischievous twin bunnies?

Would you rather
watch all your eggs float up into the sky

or watch them all suddenly
roll away downhill?

Would you rather
turn the Easter Bunny's
carrot stash into wiggly jelly

into exploding
glitter tubes?

Would you rather chase a sneaky chick who stole your Easter bonnet  a naughty bunny who borrowed your shoes and is now sprinting away with them?

Would you rather wrangle a growing whipped-cream explosion  a giant bubblegum bubble stretching bigger... and bigger... and bigger?

Would you rather hatch an egg that sprouts legs and speeds away,  an egg that spins so fast it drills a hole in the ground?

Would you rather your voice sound like a squeaky Easter basket toy  blast out like an Easter parade trumpet every time you try to say "Happy Easter?"

Would you rather shrink to bunny size for an hour,  grow as tall as the Bunny Town clock tower by accident?

Would you rather your shadow suddenly hop away on its own  start breakdancing wildly behind you?

Would you rather have shoes that fill themselves with jelly-beans  pockets that magically fill with tiny baby chicks?

Would you rather get sneezed on by a glitter-spraying bunny  by a bubble-blowing chick?

Would you rather try to stop a runaway egg parade rolling through town,  clean up after a monumental chocolate fountain explosion?

CHAPTER 8

SPRINGTIME ADVENTURES

Springtime in Easter Wonderland is more than a season; it's a celebration that never stops blossoming. The air is warm and sparkly, the breeze smells like fresh flowers, and the sky is painted in pastels that shift whenever a butterfly flaps its wings. Meadows giggle when you step on them, forests shuffle their leaves to whisper secrets, and creeks hum cheerful tunes as they wind through the land.

Every corner is a new invitation to explore, play, and discover something magical hiding beneath a petal or floating on a breeze.

Ready to step outside? Your springtime adventure awaits!

Would you rather
dive into a giant pile of soft,
warm spring blossoms  leap into a swirling mound of
rainbow-colored leaves that
smell like candy?

Would you rather
race the playful spring wind
across a meadow  splash through
glowing, magical puddles
that burst into sparkles
when you jump?

Would you rather
be followed everywhere by a
shimmering cloud
of butterflies  by tiny birds
singing a personal
theme song for you?

Would you rather
have a picnic on a floating
lily pad that gently rocks  inside a giant hollow
tree filled with glowing
firefly lanterns?

Would you rather
walk through a forest
where every tree whispers
silly jokes,  a garden where
the flowers sing cheerful
springtime songs?

Would you rather slide down a hill made of soft, mossy velvet  bounce across giant mushroom caps shaped like pastel cupcakes?

Would you rather have a friendly breeze that cools you gently wherever you go,  a tiny rain cloud that waters flowers in your footsteps?

Would you rather enjoy spring rain that hums a lullaby as it falls  sunbeams that sprinkle everything with glittery sparkles?

Would you rather go cloud-watching with a bunny who names each cloud after desserts,  with a chick who insists they all look like magical creatures?

Would you rather hike through a meadow filled with floating, tickly seed pods  one where all the plants softly glow at nighttime?

Would you rather
weave a magical flower crown that never wilts

or build a giant bird's nest sturdy
enough to sit and read in?

Would you rather
discover a secret waterfall
that rains jelly-beans

 OR

a hidden pond
where bubbles rise in fun
shapes and faces?

Would you rather talk to ladybugs that offer wise advice  frogs that speak only in rhymes?

Would you rather stroll through a forest where the path moves like a soft escalator,  a garden where stepping stones light up beneath your feet?

Would you rather help a butterfly smooth out its sparkly, tangled wings  help a squirrel sort its stash of rainbow acorns?

Would you rather wear spring boots that let you hop sky-high  sneakers that help you run twice as fast across rolling green hills?

Would you rather explore a field of bouncing dandelions  a valley where the grass giggles every time you touch it?

Would you rather ride
a giant ladybug across sunlit fields

or float peacefully on
the back of a giant turtle across a sparkling pond?

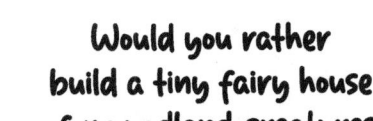

Would you rather
build a tiny fairy house
for woodland creatures

OR

a giant stick-and-flower
fort in a magical grove?

Would you rather discover a tree that grows star-shaped fruit  a bush that produces berries that glow like lanterns at night?

Would you rather befriend a deer that leaves twinkling hoofprints with every step  a fox that changes fur colors with every season?

Would you rather have a spring wind that gently lifts you during jumps,  raindrops that give you little bursts of energy when they land on you?

Would you rather find a rainbow that hums soothing music  a rainbow that sprays soft, colorful mist when touched?

Would you rather explore a gigantic enchanted hedge maze  wander through a field of flowers taller than you?

Would you rather paddle
a leaf-shaped boat along a humming stream

or fly a kite shaped
like a giant magical Easter egg?

Would you rather
swing across fields on
stretchy flower vines

OR

bounce on a seesaw
made of giant petals
that smell like vanilla?

Would you rather chase fireflies that draw glowing patterns in the sky  follow honeybees that make candy-flavored honey?

Would you rather discover a new type of magical creature hidden in the grass  a new magical plant growing in the forest?

Would you rather tend to a garden that rearranges itself every sunrise  live in a treehouse that gently shifts to follow the warmest sunlight?

Would you rather celebrate the Spring Festival with dancing, singing flowers,  with fireworks made of shimmering pollen that burst like glitter snow?

CHAPTER 9

EASTER CHALLENGES & COMPETITIONS

Welcome to the Great Easter Games Arena, the most exciting spot in all of Easter Wonderland! The fields are freshly trimmed, the banners are fluttering, and the stands are packed with cheering bunnies, clapping chicks, and glitter-tossing butterflies.

Every spring, creatures from all corners gather here for competitions filled with magic, laughter, and a whole lot of hopping. Whether you're racing bouncing eggs, building candy structures, or chasing runaway marshmallows, one thing's for sure: the challenges are wild, the prizes are sparkly, and anything can happen.

Stretch your legs, tighten your bunny ears, and get ready. The starting whistle is about to blow!

Would you rather compete in an egg-balancing race on a super windy hill  attempt a hopping marathon wearing giant, floppy bunny feet?

Would you rather enter a jelly-bean catapult contest  a chocolate-bunny stacking showdown where the bunnies keep wobbling?

Would you rather partner in a three-legged race with the super-fast Easter Bunny  with a tiny chick determined to win at all costs?

Would you rather try to catch floating eggs drifting toward the sky  chase rolling eggs zooming downhill like racers?

Would you rather build the tallest carrot tower that leans dangerously  construct the strongest candy house that keeps melting in the sun?

Would you rather
run an obstacle course filled with bouncing eggs

or tackle one filled with jelly-bean patches that act like banana peels?

Would you rather compete in a bunny-hop marathon across the meadow

OR

a chick-sprint dash where the chicks keep cheering you on?

Would you rather play soccer with an egg that randomly changes directions,  play basketball with a jelly-bean ball that keeps shrinking mid-dribble?

Would you rather go on a treasure hunt in a meadow filled with magical clues  in a maze made of giant spring flowers that move?

Would you rather stack eggs as tall as your own height  balance one enormous egg that tries its best to wiggle off your hand?

Would you rather race through an obstacle course on a bunny-powered scooter  zoom down a winding track on a chick-powered skateboard?

Would you rather enter a bubble-blowing contest where bubbles bounce like rubber balls,  a whistle challenge where each whistle summons a random magical creature?

Would you rather try
to lasso a runaway giant egg

or chase a marshmallow
that bounces higher every time you get close?

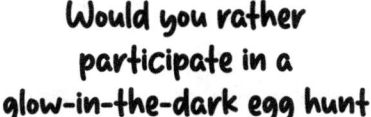

Would you rather
participate in a
glow-in-the-dark egg hunt

in a nighttime race lit by
floating fireflies forming
arrows in the sky?

Would you rather enter a carrot-juggling contest where the carrots squeak  an egg-spinning contest where the eggs vibrate when you win?

Would you rather join a team famous for super speed  a team famous for wacky but powerful magic gadgets?

Would you rather hop over giant chocolate bars in a race  crawl under swinging licorice ropes in a candy tunnel?

Would you rather solve tricky puzzles to unlock a golden egg  complete silly mini-challenges to earn sparkly egg stickers?

Would you rather do a relay race where each teammate must hop, skip, and wiggle,  one where each runner carries a magical talking egg that comments on everything?

Would you rather compete
in a rainbow rope tug-of-war

or balance on floating lily pads
that drift and spin beneath your feet?

Would you rather
try a leaf-surfing
challenge across
breezy hills

OR

a cloud-jumping contest
high above the fields?

Would you rather team up with a Bunny Town partner who never stops cheering you on with silly Easter chants  one who keeps cracking egg-cellent jokes to distract your opponents during every game?

Would you rather chase a slippery golden egg coated in magic  pop balloons filled with glittering sparkles that burst into shapes?

Would you rather win a "don't laugh" battle while bunnies tell ridiculous jokes  a "don't move" challenge while dancing chicks try to tempt you?

Would you rather choose a bravery challenge like walking through a meadow of giggling plants  a skill challenge guiding a bouncing egg through a twisty maze?

Would you rather race on a track made entirely of springy jelly  compete on a marshmallow course that sinks slightly under your feet?

Would you rather win a giant chocolate trophy bigger than your head  a magical golden egg that gives one silly surprise each morning?

Would you rather be captain of the Bunny Relay Squad  leader of the Chick Cheer Squad?

Would you rather decorate eggs while blindfolded in a speed challenge,  decorate eggs that won't stop rolling off the table?

Would you rather battle for victory in the Grand Easter Challenge, cheered by all of Easter Wonderland,  join the top-secret Silly Games known only to the bravest adventurers?

CHAPTER 10

THE BIG EASTER FINALE

At last… you've reached the heart of Easter Wonderland; the place where every magical moment from your journey comes together. As night settles in, the sky glows with swirling colors, lanterns shaped like eggs float through the air, and creatures from every corner gather in excitement.

The Great Easter Finale isn't just a celebration: it's a spectacular mix of music, magic, laughter, glowing eggs, enchanted creatures, and surprises that only appear once a year. The air tingles with energy. The ground hums. And every eye, bunny, chick, lamb, and more, turns toward you.

You aren't just a visitor anymore. You're part of the story. Part of the celebration. Part of the magic.

Tonight, Easter Wonderland opens its gates for its grandest event, and YOU get to decide how your adventure ends.

Would you rather
receive your final mission
from the Easter Bunny
in person

 **OR**

from the ancient Golden Egg
that glows brighter
the closer you get?

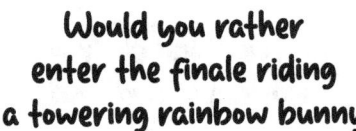

Would you rather
enter the finale riding
a towering rainbow bunny

 **OR**

floating on a shimmering
egg-shaped airship?

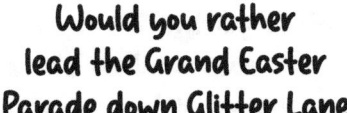

Would you rather
lead the Grand Easter
Parade down Glitter Lane

 **OR**

conduct the legendary
orchestra of singing chicks
and humming eggs?

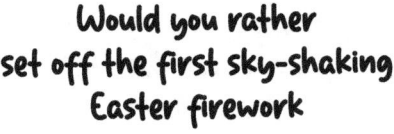

Would you rather
set off the first sky-shaking
Easter firework

 **OR**

reveal the Grand Egg that
changes colors with the
crowd's cheers?

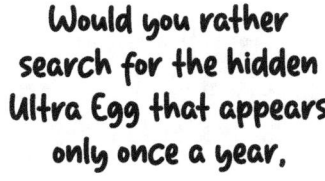

Would you rather
search for the hidden
Ultra Egg that appears
only once a year,

 **OR**

guard it from playful
creatures who desperately
want to peek inside?

89

Would you rather solve the riddle that unlocks the Easter Treasure Chamber  follow a glowing trail that leads to a surprise no one has ever seen?

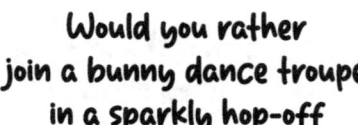

Would you rather join a bunny dance troupe in a sparkly hop-off  join the chick choir in a musical showdown?

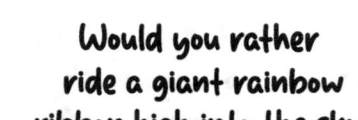

Would you rather ride a giant rainbow ribbon high into the sky  float gently downward on a marshmallow cloud sprinkled with stardust?

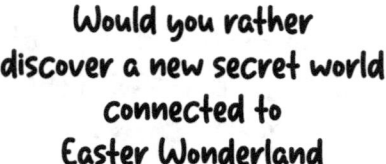

Would you rather discover a new secret world connected to Easter Wonderland  uncover a forgotten landmark deep in Bunny Town?

Would you rather meet the very first magical creature ever born in Easter Wonderland,  meet the newest creature that hatched during the Finale?

Would you rather decorate
the enormous Legendary Finale Egg with glowing magic paint

or enchant it so it lights up
whenever anyone laughs?

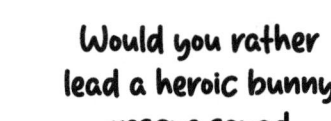

Would you rather
lead a heroic bunny
rescue squad

command an elite team
of clever, fast-thinking
chicks?

Would you rather carry the magical Spring Crystal across a cheering crowd  present it onstage as fireworks burst all around you?

Would you rather discover a portal showing other Easter worlds  learn the secret ability to create tiny portals of your own?

Would you rather help the Easter Bunny test a top-secret invention that might work,  help a magical creature unlock a new hidden power?

Would you rather stop a giant runaway egg rolling straight toward the festival  chase a glitter storm that escaped from the firework launchers?

Would you rather catch pastel fireworks that transform into candy when they fall,  catch flower petals that turn into glowing butterflies?

Would you rather be chosen to crown
the champion of the Grand Easter Games

or be crowned the Spring Hero
of Easter Wonderland?

Would you rather
relight the glowing Easter
egg archway that's fading
during the celebration,

OR

repair the magical
Easter fountain that's
supposed to spray
rainbow-colored egg-dye
but suddenly sputtered out?

Would you rather
lead a lantern march
through the glowing gardens

a sparkling egg parade
through Bunny Town
Square?

Would you rather
receive a locked egg
that hums softly
with mystery

an unlocked egg
full of unpredictable
magical surprises?

Would you rather
discover you can hop
as high as the
bursting fireworks

run as fast as
the shooting stars
streaking overhead?

Would you rather
have your magical creature
sidekick join you onstage

team up with
the Easter Bunny for
the grand finale?

Would you rather
end the night with
a giant chocolate statue
made in your honor

a burst of confetti
clouds that spell
your name in the sky?

Would you rather explore a glowing Easter-egg cavern
that only appears during the Finale,

or climb a giant sprouting beanstalk leading
to a floating garden full of magical painted eggs?

Would you rather
direct the Grand Easter
Finale with shimmering
bunny-lantern lights

OR

design the giant Egg of the
Year that appears during
the last moment?

Would you rather receive a magical egg that gives a tiny wish each day,  a basket that always fills itself with exactly what you need most?

Would you rather see constellations shaped like hopping bunnies fill the night sky,  see floating fireworks forming giant jelly-bean patterns?

Would you rather join the Big Easter Feast as the guest of honor  explore the glowing, transformed gardens after everyone else goes to sleep?

Would you rather be invited back every year as a beloved guest of Easter Wonderland  return as one of the official creators of next year's Easter magic?

CONCLUSION

Thank you for hopping through Would You Rather? Easter Edition and bringing Easter Wonderland to life with your imagination!

Throughout these pages, you've raced through windy meadows, survived glitter tornadoes, decorated eggs with magical mischief, befriended fantastical creatures, outsmarted runaway chocolates, and helped shape the Grand Easter Finale itself. Not everyone gets invited on such an adventure, but you did, and you made it unforgettable.

Every choice you made created a new possibility, a new story, a new spark of magic. That's the true wonder of Easter: it celebrates surprises, creativity, and the joy of discovering something new around every corner. And with every silly scenario you explored, you added a little more laughter, color, and light to the world of Easter Wonderland.

Even though this book is ending, the fun doesn't have to stop. You can take this spirit of curiosity with you wherever you go. Dream up your own silly choices. Invent new magical creatures. Imagine new adventures waiting just beyond the next page.

Because Easter Wonderland isn't just a place in a book; it's a world you helped build, and one you can return to anytime simply by letting your imagination hop free.

So as you close this book, keep smiling, keep wondering, and keep choosing the adventures that make your heart feel bright.

Happy Easter, and may your days be filled with color, kindness, and wonderfully silly "Would You Rather?" moments!

DID YOU ENJOY THE BOOK?

If you did, we are ecstatic. If not, please write your complaint to us and we will ensure we fix it.

If you're feeling generous, there is something important that you can help me with - tell other people that you enjoyed the book.

Ask a grown-up to write about it on Amazon. When they do, more people will find out about the book. It also lets Amazon know that we are making kids around the world laugh. Even a few words and ratings would go a long way.

If you have any ideas or jokes that you think are super funny, please let us know. We would love to hear from you. Our email address is -

riddleland@riddlelandforkids.com

ABOUT RIDDLELAND

Riddleland is a mum + dad run publishing company. We are passionate about creating fun and innovative books to help children develop their reading skills and fall in love with reading. If you have suggestions for us or want to work with us, shoot us an email at riddleland@riddlelandforkids.com

Our family's favorite quote:

"Creativity is an area in which younger people have a tremendous advantage since they have an endearing habit of always questioning past wisdom and authority."

~ Bill Hewlett